Sea Otters In Valdez Alaska

Sea Otters In Valdez Alaska

BOB BENDA

Sea Otters In Valdez Alaska

BOB BENDA

In February and March many sea otters moved into the Valdez Small Boat Harbor. There were as many as thirty there at one time. They swam in the water and fed on shellfish and starfish. They also hauled out on the ice to rest or sleep. I was able to watch and photograph them for several weeks as they interacted with each other. This photo shows three sea otters hauled out on the ice behind a sailboat.

These two sea otters are sitting on the ice. Their warm body heat will cause their fur to freeze to the surface of the ice if they don't move around. I saw one otter on the floating dock with its fur stuck in the ice. I splashed buckets of seawater on it so it could free itself from the ice.

As the air temperature drops thicker sheets of ice form. This photo shows three sea otters standing up in shallow water between sheets of ice. Ocean water freezes at a lower temperature than fresh water. Several of the city storm water pipes empty into the small boat harbor. This storm water dilutes the ocean water lowering its salt content so it freezes.

Here's another otter floating on its back in open water between ice sheets. This otter is eating mussels that live in the small boat harbor. Empty mussel shells are scattered on the ice sheet by the otter.

This is another sea otter eating mussels in a nearby open water area. The otter dives down and collects the mussels. The sea otter has a loose pouch of skin under each foreleg that extends across the chest. The otter usually stores food in the left pouch and brings it to the surface. The otter puts the shells on its chest and eats them one at a time.

Here's another sea otter in the ice sheet area. It caught a starfish on the bottom of the small boat harbor. Sea otters eat starfish one false foot (the star-like appendage) at a time.

Sometimes ice formed over most of the small boat harbor. When the sea otters foraged they would break an opening in the thinner ice. This allowed them to breathe and feed. Broken pieces of thin ice surround the hole it made.

One evening my son called me and said the sea otters were hauled out on the ice in the small boat harbor. He knew I had been photographing them during the day and thought maybe I wanted to photograph them at night. This photo shows eleven sea otters hauled out. This was in one section with few boats. There were more otters scattered around this area.

Here are thirteen more sea otters in another area
of the small boat harbor. There are more boats
docked behind this open area. This means less
ice for the otters to haul out on.

The next day I was walking on one of the floating docks. I photographed this sea otter resting on the snow covered ice. It watched me as I walked along the floating dock.

I stopped to take more pictures. It started moving away from me. It must have thought I was getting too close.

It took off running through the snow. The large back fins were throwing snow into the air as it headed for the water.

It reached the end of the ice and started diving onto the water. I was amazed at how quickly it moved over the snow covered ice.

This is a large sea otter on the edge of the ice. It was a sunny day and it was just resting. You can see how thick its fur is. When their fur dries the otters look much larger on land than they do in the water. Sea otters have no blubber and rely on their dense fur to keep warm. In adults, the head, throat, and chest fur are lighter (grizzled) in color.

During warmer weather male and female sea otters tend to rest together in single-sex groups called rafts. This gathering of otters in the small boat harbor was probably a mix of adult males and females. Some of the smaller otters may have been juveniles. This photo shows four otters. Two are grooming their fur and two are floating and resting. Because otters have a very loose skin and supple skeleton they can groom fur on any part of their body.

This otter has grizzled fur on its head. It's just floating and resting in the water. When sea otters are not feeding they are either sleeping, resting or grooming their fur.

This otter was sleeping on one of the floating docks. It didn't seem to be bothered by me taking its picture. It would close its eyes and sleep in the sun then wake up to look at me. I spent 30 minutes watching it from about 15 feet away.

The otters weren't always feeding, sleeping, resting, or grooming. This is one of several photos I took of these two otters fighting each other. They were both floating in the water with ice chunks near them. One of them decided to climb on the other one.

The otter stopped climbing on the other otter and dove under it. It splashed water over the other otter's head when it dove.

They came up together and started to fight with each other.

Now they really went after each other. There was water splashing all over the area.

One of the otters was pushing the other one underwater. They seemed to be really fighting with each other.

They both came to the surface and looked at each other. Then they stopped fighting and swam away from each other. This was the first time I ever saw sea otters fighting. I felt fortunate to have been able to photograph them.

This sea otter was foraging in an open water area. It had just finished eating and was grooming its fore paws.

After it finished cleaning its fore paws it dove down to collect more food. It dives head first and propels itself underwater using its large hind fins and muscular tail.

This photo shows the power of the hind fins and the tail as the otter dives down to forage on the bottom.

This sea otter managed to capture a starfish. As I said before the otter eats one false foot at a time. They dive under water and surface again to eat another false foot. They do this several times until the starfish is devoured.

This is not a great photo, but it shows an otter that captured a crab. They use their flat molars to crush the shell-like exoskeleton of the crab.

This otter was swimming on its back. Swimming on their back is their preferred method of loco-motion. It moves like this by sculling its hind feet and tail from side to side. You can see the two upper incisors. Seals and sea otter are the only carnivores with two pairs of lower incisors.

The sea otters spent five weeks in the small boat harbor before they swam out into Port Valdez. This picture shows what they left behind on the remaining ice. They also left similar deposits on the floating docks and fingers. I had to be careful when I walked around taking pictures.

I was able to photograph sea otters at the Solomon Gulch Fish Hatchery in late summer and early fall. This photo shows an otter eating a salmon head.

This large Glaucous-winged seagull seems to be interested in what the sea otter is eating. During the salmon runs sea otters, harbor seals, sea lions, seagulls, and bears feed on the fish.

This is the same otter that was eating the salmon head. Now it's holding a piece of salmon in its paws.

In late fall the sea otters would feed below the Solomon Gulch waterfall. Here is a mother sea otter with her juvenile pup. The pup was born in the spring. The mother otter rears the pup and teaches it how to forage for food.

This otter has the gills from a salmon. It was probably left by the bears and seals that were feeding in this area.

This immature seagull seems interested in the piece of salmon the sea otter is eating.

The otter now has a salmon head to eat.

It dives under the water holding the salmon in its paws. You can see how its groomed fur repels the water.

As winter approaches the snow starts falling. This sea otter got a nose covered with snow foraging for food along the shoreline.

No sea otter book would be complete without a photo of an otter pup. This photo was taken during the 1989 Exxon Valdez oil spill sea otter rescue operation. The Exxon Valdez Oil Spill Trustee Council estimated 2650 otters (40% of the population) died during the oil spill. Sea otters exposed to the oil died from hypothermia, drowning, or ingesting oil toxins while grooming their fur. The population is now considered recovered.

ALASKA SEA OTTER FACT SHEET

1. Ninety percent (90%) of the world's sea otters (*Enhydra lutris*) live in Alaska's coastal waters. In 1973 the sea otter population was estimated to be between 100,000 and 125,000. By 2006 it had fallen to an estimated 73,000.Most of the decline occurred in the Aleutian Islands.

2. Sea otters are the heaviest member of the weasel family. They are also the second smallest marine mammal. The smallest marine mammal is the marine otter (*Lontra felina*) of the South American coast.

3. Adult sea otters weigh between 31-99 pounds (14-45 kg) and are between 4-5feet (1.2-1.5 m) in length. Some specimens have weighed up to 119 pounds (54 kg).

4. Sea otters do not have blubber to keep warm. Instead they have the densest fur in the animal kingdom, ranging from 250,000 to a million hairs per square inch.

5. Sea otters are a keystone species (meaning they have a greater role in their environment than other species).

6. Sea otters eat urchins, abalone, mussels, crabs, snails and about 40 other marine species. Sea otter teeth are adapted for crushing these hard-shelled invertebrates. In order to maintain its body weight and high metabolism for warmth, a sea otter must eat 25% of its body weight per day.

7. Sea otters can dive up to 330 feet (100m). It can hold its breath for up to five minutes, but its dives typically last about one minute and no more than four. They are diurnal and forage, rest, and groom from sunrise to sunset. Time spent each day foraging ranges from 24 to 60% depending on food availability in the area.

8. Sea otters use rocks to open hard shells by pounding its prey on its chest. It is one of the few mammal species to use tools.

9. Female otters reach sexual maturity at 2-5 years of age. Males mature at 4-6 years of age. Alaska sea otters give birth in May and June. Female otters usually give birth to one cub at a time. Pup nurse for 4 to 12 months in Alaska. After weaning the pup is almost as large as its mother. The pup's fur is replaced by adult fur after about 13 weeks. Female sea otter perform all tasks of feeding and rearing the pup and have occasionally been observed caring for orphaned cubs.
10. Pup mortality is high, especially during the individuals first winter. One estimate is that only 25% of pups survive their first year.
11. Sea otters tend to rest together in single-sex groups called rafts. Although sea otters can be playful and sociable, they are not considered to be truly sociable animals. They spend much time alone meeting their own needs.
12. The average life span in the wild is 23 years.

Additional information can be found at: www.adfg.alaska. gov>...>Animals

www.ingramcontent.com/pod-product-compliance
Lightning Source LLC
Chambersburg PA
CBHW050755290526
45792CB00008B/2187